ORCHESTRATION
handbook

by Don B. Ray, M.A.

Music Supervisor, ret.

CBS Television

—

Creator/Coordinator

Film Music Program

UCLA Department of the Arts

Creative Direction by Kristen Schilo, Gato & Maui Productions
Design by Lisa Vaughn, Two of Cups Design Studio, Inc.

ISBN: 0-634-01311-4

HAL•LEONARD® CORPORATION
7777 W. BLUEMOUND RD. P.O. BOX 13819 MILWAUKEE, WI 53213

Visit Hal Leonard Online at
www.halleonard.com

FOREWORD

There is surprisingly little agreement on the playable outer limits of many instruments, as a performer's skill affects range; obviously there is considerable latitude in technique between a freshman instrumentalist and an experienced studio or symphony musician. In the case of brass instruments, the practical upper limit is further modified by the manner in which it is approached; if led up to by step and at good volume, the upper limit is extended slightly and will be dependably negotiated. If approached by a wide leap and/or at soft volume, the upper limit becomes more problematic.

This guide then represents a consensus of what composers may realistically expect if they do not have virtuoso instrumentalists available to them.

For those requiring a more thorough reference to orchestral instruments, please refer to Kennan's *The Technique of Orchestration*, Piston's *Orchestration* or Garner Reed's *Thesaurus of Orchestral Devices*. Those needing a comprehensive dictionary of musical terms should refer to the *Harvard Dictionary of Music* or the concise *Elson's Pocket Music Dictionary*.

The various lists of tempi, volumes and mood indications are not intended to be comprehensive, merely a quick reference.

All ranges listed in this guide are actual pitches.

CONTENTS

ORCHESTRATION
handbook

winds

—

saxophones

—

brass

—

PICCOLO IN C

Range:

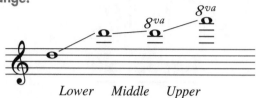

Lower   Middle   Upper

Clef: treble

Transposition: sounds an octave higher than written

Timbre:

Lower range: good but unexploited register; poor projection

Middle range: good quality and control

Upper range: penetrating and brilliant

General characteristics:
* agile and requires little breath
* intonation can be a problem

Special effects:

Flutter: A sound produced on one pitch similar in quality to the cooing of a dove, indicated thus:

Trill: Rapid alternation between written note and neighboring upper note of scale (if music is tonal). Otherwise an accidental at right of sign indicates whether upper note is sharp, natural or flat; indicated thus:

Wider trills between non-adjoining notes are indicated thus:

1

FLUTE

Range:

Low   Middle Upper High

Clef: treble

Transposition: sounds as written

Timbre:
Low range: dark, haunting sound
Middle range: sonorous quality but poor projection
Upper range: bright, carrying sound
High range: bright, penetrating quality

Characteristics:
- very agile throughout range
- the lower the register, the more breath required

Special effects: same as piccolo

ALTO FLUTE

Range:

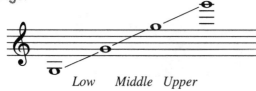

Low   Middle   Upper

Clef: treble

Transposition: sounds a perfect fourth lower than written

Timbre:
Low range: haunting, throaty, soft
Middle range: rich, throaty sound
Upper range: good quality; projects

Characteristics: same as flute, but uses considerably more breath

Special effects: same as piccolo except that flutter is ineffective in low and middle registers

OBOE

Range:

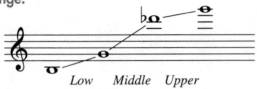

Low   Middle   Upper

Clef: treble

Transposition: sounds as written

Timbre:
Lower range: rich, exotic sound; difficult to play softly
Middle range: characteristic color
Upper range: thin and tentative near top; loses volume

Characteristics:
- very agile throughout register
- requires little breath
- particularly expressive instrument

Special effects: see piccolo: Special Effects: Trills

ENGLISH HORN

Range:

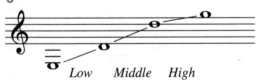

Low   Middle   High

Clef: treble

Transposition: sounds a perfect fifth lower than written

Timbre:
Low range: dark, sensuous sound; difficult to play softly
Middle range: like oboe but more resonant
Upper range: like oboe but more projected sound

Characteristics: same as oboe; less agile

Special effects: see piccolo: Special Effects: Trills

CLARINET IN B♭

1

Range:

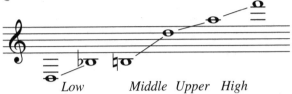

Low   *Middle*   *Upper*   *High*

Clef: treble

Transposition: sounds a whole step lower than written

Timbre:
Low range: rich throaty sound
Middle range: not much projection
Upper range: bright; good projection
High range: shrill, penetrating

Characteristics: good volume control except in lowest register, which also requires considerable breath

Special effects:
Sub-tone: a soft, whispered tone; best in low and mid-register
Trill: see piccolo: Special Effects
Glissando: ascending glissando possible; best in upper register

CLARINET IN A

Note: Same as clarinet in B♭ except that range is half-step lower and instrument sounds a minor third lower than written. Rarely used today, although common in nineteenth–century French music.

CLARINET IN E♭

Note: Same as clarinet in B♭ except that fundamental is a fourth higher. E♭ clarinet sounds a minor third higher than written.

BASS CLARINET IN B♭

Range:

Low   *Upper*

Clef: treble *only*

Transposition: sounds a major ninth lower than written

Timbre:
Low range: dark, resonant, haunting
Upper range: bright, projective

Characteristics:
- requires considerable breath, especially in low register
- quite agile, considering range
- a haunting melody instrument

Special effects:
Trills: see piccolo: Special Effects
Glissando: upward glissandi are eerily effective; check with player for best range

CONTRA-ALTO CLARINET IN E♭

Range: **Clef:** treble

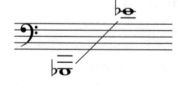

Transposition: sounds an octave and a major-sixth lower than written

Timbre: harsh, penetrating quality

Characteristics: same as B♭ bass clarinet

Special effects: same as B♭ bass clarinet

Note: This is commonly mistaken for the E♭ contrabass clarinet which is actually another (and even-rarer) instrument.

BASSOON

Range:

Clefs: treble (rare), tenor and bass

Transposition: sounds as written

Timbre:
Low range: dark, resonant, projective
Middle range: characteristic sound
Upper range: soft, sensuous, poor projection

Characteristics:
- low range requires considerable breath
- considering range, quite agile
- a haunting melody instrument

Special effects: Trills: See piccolo: Special Effects

CONTRA BASSOON

Range:

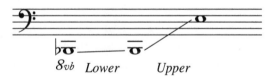

Clef: bass

Transposition: sounds an octave lower than written

Timbre:
Lower range: low, growling sound, but surprisingly good pitch focus
Upper range: same quality as bassoon

Characteristics:
- requires considerable breath throughout range
- not as agile as the bassoon
- difficult to play quietly, especially the lower registers

Special effects: Trills: see piccolo: Special Effects

SOPRANO SAXOPHONE IN B♭

Range: **Clef:** treble

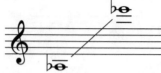

Transposition: sounds a whole step lower than written

Timbre: fairly even throughout range although slightly raucous in lowest register and slightly pinched in top range; similar in sound to English horn (not characteristic sax sound)

Characteristics:
- agile throughout range; requires little breath except in lower range
- intonation is a major problem
- blends poorly to other winds
- two performance traditions:
  Popular: breathy, sensuous or rather raucous; exaggerated vibrato; considerable liberties with melodic line
  Classical: same discipline as any other wind instruments

Special effects:

Trill: Rapid alternation between written and neighboring upper note of scale, if music is tonal; otherwise an accidental is placed to right of trill sign (Tr.) to indicate whether upper note is sharp, natural or flat; indicated as follows:

Wider trills (when mechanically possible) are indicated thus:

ALTO SAXOPHONE IN E♭

1

Range: **Clef:** treble

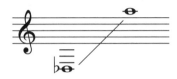

Transposition: sounds a major-sixth lower than written

Timbre: even throughout range; characteristic saxophone quality

Characteristics:
- agile throughout rage; requires little breath
- blends poorly with other instruments
- two performance traditions:
  Popular: breathy, sensuous or rather raucous; exaggerated vibrato; considerable liberties with melodic lines
  Classical: as disciplined as any other wind instrument

Special effects:
Sub-tone: a quiet, mellow sound (indicated by writing "sub-tone" at beginning of passage)
While the saxophone cannot flutter a tone or slide between pitches, it can "bend" notes a little, at player's option. It can also produce a "growl."
Trills: see soprano saxophone: Special Effects

TENOR SAXOPHONE IN B♭

Range: **Clef:** treble

Transposition: sounds a major-ninth lower than written

Timbre: even throughout range

Characteristics: same as alto saxophone

Special effects: same as alto saxophone

BARITONE SAXOPHONE IN E♭

Range: **Clef:** treble

Transposition: sounds an octave and a major-sixth lower than written

Timbre: fairly even throughout range although rather harsh and projective in lower register

Characteristics:
- considering register, surprisingly agile; requires substantial breath
- blends poorly with other winds but can be an effective underpinning for a brass chord
- two performance traditions:
  Popular: Rather raucous sound; exaggerated vibrato; considerable liberties with melody lines
  Classical: As disciplined as any other wind instrument

Special effects: same as alto saxophone

BASS SAXOPHONE IN B♭

Range: **Clef:** treble

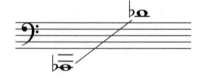

Transposition: sounds two octaves and a major-second lower than written

Timbre: somewhat tubbier sound than that of baritone saxophone

Characteristics: same as baritone saxophone except for more intonation problems

Special effects: see baritone saxophone

Note: not too many of these exist now; be sure of availability before using

FRENCH HORN

1

Range:

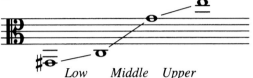

Low   Middle   Upper

Clef: alto

Transposition: sounds a fifth lower than written

Timbre:
Low range: dark, tuba-like; no volume
Middle range: rich, controlled sound
Upper range: brilliant, epic-like quality

Characteristics:
- upper limit should be approached by step and at good volume, otherwise results can be shaky
- low range requires much breath and has little volume; better with two players on part
- continuous playing in one register tires embouchure; move players around and allow breaks between passages
- brass muting and hand muting wear down embouchure; use sparingly

Special effects:
Trills: see piccolo: Special Effects
Glissando: a brief, explosive upward gliss is possible in upper register; effective but wearing
Cuivré: A brassy sound achieved via increased lung pressure and embouchure tension; available on muted or open horn. When returning to normal production, indicate "normal" tone.
Sordino (muting):
  Straight mute: produces a soft mellow sound
  Brass mute: produces a nasal, sinister sound
  Hand-muting: produces a thin, distant, rather-sinister sound; very wearing on embouchure; often indicated by a plus sign (+) over notes to be muted

TRUMPET IN B♭

Range:

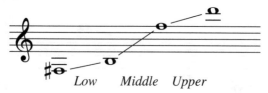

Low   Middle   Upper

Clef: treble

Transposition: sounds a whole step lower than written

Timbre:

Low range: dark, effective; some intonation problems; poor projection

Middle range: best range; good control of volume, intonation, color, etc.

Upper range: brilliant, penetrating

Characteristics:
- agile throughout range
- wide expressive capability
- lower range requires some breath

Special effects:

Trills: see piccolo: Special Effects

Shake: In modern usage, a rapid alternation of loud to soft on same note; like flutter on flute, indicated by wavy line over note. Very wearing; use sparingly.

Sordino (muting):
  Bucket (or hand over bell): a soft mellow effect
  Straight mute: soft mellow sound
  Cup mute: mellow, soft, metallic
  Harmon mute: thin, very metallic

TRUMPET IN C

a non-transposing trumpet somewhat mellower than the B♭ trumpet; range is a full step higher

TRUMPET IN D

a bright timbre; sounds a step higher than written; range is a third higher than B♭ trumpet

FLEUGEL HORN

range, transposition same as B♭ trumpet but most effective in low register; very mellow character; the fluegel horn cannot accomodate mutes

B♭ PICCOLO TRUMPET

a thin, toy-like sound having considerable tension; sounds a minor-seventh higher than written; range from A above middle-C to high-C

TENOR TROMBONE

Range:

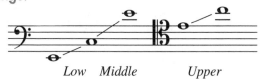

Low   Middle   Upper

Clefs: bass and tenor (not treble)

Transposition: sounds as written

Timbre:
Low range: tubby but good pitch focus
Middle range: good quality and control
Upper range: brilliant, penetrating

Characteristics:
- uses considerable breath
- below middle-C, legato style difficult
- fast-moving passages are unidiomatic

Special effects:

Trills: rarely used and not effective

Shake: see trumpet: Special effects

Glissando: the sliding mechanism allows some hair-raising effects; see below for glissandi that are possible

Sordino: see trumpet: Special effects

The Slide Mechanism

Two factors control pitch; length of tubing (slide position) and lip tension (embouchure), the latter affecting which overtone or fundamental will be produced. In first position (shortest tube length), the follow pitches can be excited:

(pedal)

In second position, the following will be produced (depending on lip tension):

(pedal)

Depending on slide position, the following 1st overtones can be induced (parentheses indicate slide position):

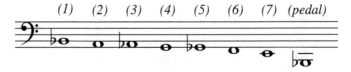

2nd Overtone:

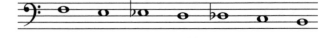

3rd Overtone:

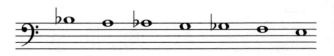

4th Overtone:

5th Overtone:

Note: Only pedal tones in 1st and 2nd positions (low B^b and low A) are useful; the others take too much breath and have poor pitch definition.

BASS TROMBONE

Range:

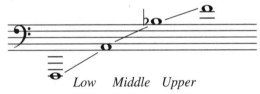

Low   Middle   Upper

Clef: bass

Transposition: sounds as written

Timbre:
Low register: more edge than tuba
Middle range: characteristic quality
Upper range: bright projective sound

Characteristics: The bass trombone is effectively a double instrument, allowing it a variety of options not available on tenor trombone; so bass trombone is more flexible in center of range than tenor trombone.

Special effects: see tenor trombone

TUBA

Range:

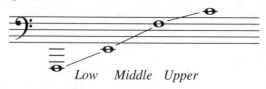

Low   Middle   Upper

Clef: bass

Transposition: sounds as written

Timbre:

Low range: dark mellow timbre; good pitch focus but uses breath rapidly (one bar in moderate 4/4 is about maximum)

Middle range: full-bodied, velvety

Upper range: projective, sonorous

Characteristics:

- a cousin of the French horn, the tuba has a mellower sound than a bass trombone in the same register
- good control of dynamics except in extremes of range
- considering register, surprisingly agile
- there are a variety of tubas with a variety of fundamentals, but all are non-transposing and all have similar ranges
- tuba players complain that composers fail to exploit possibilities of instrument, both in range and flexibility

Special effects:

Sordino: the only mute generally available is straight mute

- shakes and glissandi are not practical on tuba
- trills are possible but ineffective except in upper register; see piccolo: Special effects

ORCHESTRATION
handbook

guitars

—

keyboards

—

harp

—

pitched percussion

—

unpitched percussion

—

voices

—

ACOUSTIC (CLASSICAL) GUITAR

Range: **Clef:** treble

Open strings:

Transposition: sounds an octave lower than written

Timbre: fairly even throughout range although decay of tone is slower in low register

Characteristics:
- an idiosyncratic instrument one must really play to understand; lacking this, composer should write what he wants, then check out the part with a guitar player
- two performance styles:
  Classical: where player plays exactly what is written, usually a one- or two-line part with occasional chords
  Popular: where player improvises within framework indicated by composer:

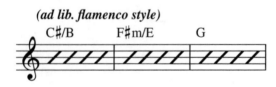

Special effects: A variety of sounds and figures are available that are so special that the composer should consult a player for guidance.

ELECTRIC GUITAR

Note: Has same range as classical guitar (plus a few higher notes) but decay is dramatically slower. Recently a variety of electronic sound-modifiers (phase shifters, digital delay, etc.) have been introduced which produce exotic, spacey sounds; again see player.

ELECTRIC BASS

Range: **Clef:** bass

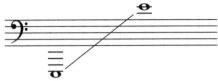

Open Strings:

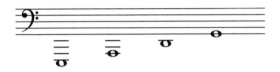

Transposition: sounds an octave lower than written

Timbre: good volume control throughout range; pitch becomes diffused in lowest fourth of range

Characteristics:
- decay is so slow that instrument may be described as a sustaining instrument
- electric bass can be very agile, recently, some young bassists have effectively redefined the instrument by using it chordally, creating intricate figures that outline chords
- two performance styles:
  Classical: where player plays exactly what is written
  Popular: where player improvises within a framework indicated by the composer:

or:

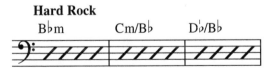

Special effects: Sound can be modified by such electronic devices as phase shifters, fuzz tone, digital delays, ring modulators, etc. producing "spacey" exotic effects.

PIANO

Range:

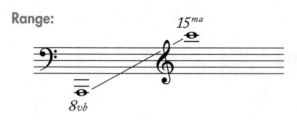

Clefs: treble, bass (double-stave part)

Transposition: sounds as written

Timbre: even throughout range

Special effects: sustaining pedal activated by "Ped" written below note or passage

CELESTE

Range:

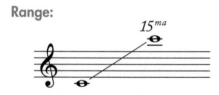

Clef: treble

Transposition: sounds an octave higher than written

Timbre: a soft, bell-like sound that is even throughout range and has surprising carrying power

HARPSICHORD

Range:

Clef: treble, bass (double-stave part)

Transposition: sounds as written

Timbre: even throughout range

Characteristics:
- a plucked keyboard instrument, the lower register sustains considerably longer than upper range
- there is great variety between instruments in color, stops (doublings) and sound projection. Also there are electric harpsichords as well as acoustical; these are normally less satisfying aurally than acoustic models but tend to stay in tune better.

CLAVINET

Range:

Clefs: treble, bass (double-stave part)

Transposition: sounds as written

Timbre: an electronic keyboard instrument with a nasal, harpsichord-like sound; effective with rock-music instruments

Characteristics: basic sound can be modified some electronically, but it is primarily a one-color instrument

Note: This keyboard instrument was popular in 1983 when the *Orchestration Handbook* was first written. Today it is rarely used.

FENDER-RHODES PIANO

Range:

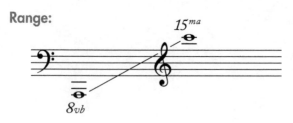

Clefs: treble, bass (double-stave part)

Transposition: sounds as written

Timbre: electronically-produced tone between that of piano and marimba (note: there are both 73 and 88-key models)

Characteristics, Special effects: same as piano

ACCORDION

Range:

Clefs: treble, bass (double or single-system)

Transposition: sounds as written

Timbre: modern accordion can produce many colors, depending on model and make

POLYPHONIC SYNTHESIZERS, ELECTRONIC ORGAN

There is such a proliferation in this field as well a such variety of colors within different models of the same brand that the reader should seek a demonstration of any instrument in which he is interested.

HARP

Range:

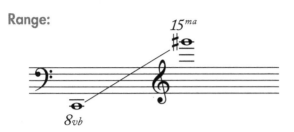

Clefs: treble, bass (double stave)

Transposition: sounds as written

Timbre:
- volume controllable throughout range
- tone decays more rapidly as one moves toward upper register

Characteristics:
- Chromatic pitch mechanism: harp strings match white notes on piano with every C connected to one foot pedal, every D connected to another, and so on. Each pedal can raise or lower its note a half-step, making rapid chromatic half-step motion impossible.
- Several notational systems exist to indicate which pedal positions to adjust, but harpists usually prefer to do this for themselves. The one thing the composer must do is be sure that the chromatics are not altered faster than the harpist can pedal the changes.
- notated like a piano part except for glissando and arpeggio figures
- as small finger is not used, five-note chords on one hand are not possible
- in orchestral writing, it is wise to double a significant harp line at the lower octave for reinforcement

Special effects:

Harmonics: A soft attractive timbre (possible only one note at a time), these sound an octave higher than written and are notated thus:

Glissandi: Easy and effective, either loud or soft, on all major, minor or whole-tone scales. There are many ways to indicate these, but possibly the simplest is the following:

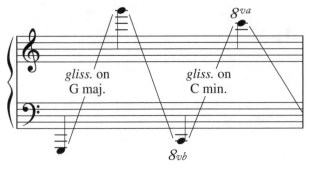

(Note: irregular glissandi can be written out, of course.)

Arpeggios: Also easy and effective, on all major, minor, diminished and augmented chords. Again, if irregular, these can be written out; but if conventional, the following notation is clear and simple:

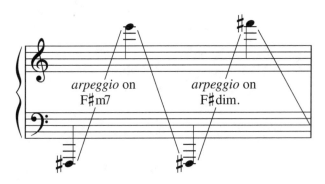

ELECTRIFIED HARP

In the last two decades, an electronically amplified harp has appeared which takes its signal directly from the sounding board. This allows for a more "present" sound. Also, sound-modifying devices are available to alter the basic harp sound.

VIBRAPHONE

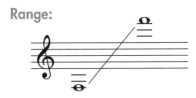

Range: **Clef:** treble

Transposition: sounds as written

Timbre: A mellow, metallic sound with good resonance and sustaining quality

Characteristics: an agile, versatile instrument effective as chordal support to another instrument, as a melody instrument or as a coloristic enhancer of another orchestra color

Special effects:
- choice of mallet allows either a mellow or hard sound; vibrato controlled by variable-speed motor
- white-note glissandi are common

MARIMBA

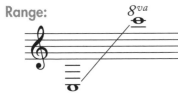

Range: **Clef:** treble

Transposition: sounds as written

Timbre: a hollow, wood-on-wood tone; more resonant in lower register

Characteristics: a capable melody instrument; also effective when used to add inconspicuous accent to other melody lines; it can also produce four-note chords

Special effects: Because of the rapid decay of sound, the only way to sustain a note (or a chord) is to roll them, produce the characteristic marimba sound, indicated thus:

XYLOPHONE

Range: **Clef:** treble

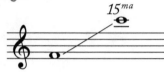

Transposition: sounds an octave higher than written

Timbre: non-resonant wood-on-wood quality

Characteristics: sound decays almost immediately

Special effects: see marimba: Special effects

GLOCKENSPIEL (ORCHESTRAL BELLS)

Range: **Clef:** treble

Transposition: sounds two octaves higher than written

Timbre: high, penetrating metal-on-metal sound; choice of mallet effects tone

Characteristics: Effective loud or soft; can penetrate the heaviest orchestral tutti. Decay is so slow it seems to continue indefinitely.

CHIMES (TUBULAR BELLS)

Range: **Clef:** treble

Transposition: sounds as written

Timbre: mellow, resonant metallic sound

Characteristics: effective loud or soft; decay is so slow that sound seems continuous

TYMPANI

Range:

| 32" | 29" | 26" | 23" | 20" |

(Note: 32" tym. means a tympani with a 32"-diameter head.)

Clef: bass

Transposition: sounds an octave lower than written (although there is some argument about this)

Timbre: on each tympani, lower end tends to sound tubby, upper end pinched

Characteristics:
- most tympani have pedal mechanisms to alter pitch, but this is difficult to do while playing; allow eight to ten bars rest for pitch changes, if unavoidable
- plastic drumheads produce bright sound but cowhide produces mellower, more musical sound
- tympani sound is modified by hardness of mallet

Special effects:

Roll: Rapid repeated notes on the same drum produces an agitated, repeated effect, effective loud or soft, indicated as follows:

Glissando: Rolled portamentos are effective and easy on pedal tympani, either up or down, loud or soft, and limited only by the range of specific tympani being used. Indicated as follows:

gliss.

EXOTIC PITCHED PERCUSSION

There are many pitched percussion instruments (boobams, timbales, etc.), but none are in general use. If an exotic instrument is required, contact owner and discuss characteristics, range, etc.

UNPITCHED PERCUSSION

(normally written without a clef sign)

Castanets

Description: two pieces of wood small enough to fit in the palm of a hand and activated by the fingers into rapid, rhythmical patterns

Timbre: sharp, wood-on-wood sound

Cymbals (Piatti)

Description: two circular brass discs (16″ to 22″ in diameter) that are struck together

Timbre: played softly, cymbals add an exotic element; at full volume they provide a brilliant accent

Cymbals, Suspended

Description: a single metal disc (18″ to 24″ in diameter) suspended from its center by a leather chord

Timbre: struck with a tympani stick, it sounds like a small gong; struck with a snare stick, it sound like piatti

Bass Drum

Description: a large drum with double heads, 30″ to 60″ in diameter, and 12″ to 24″ deep; struck with a padded mallet (beater)

Timbre: a low-pitched sound, effective loud or soft

Field Drum (or Tenor Drum)

Description: double-headed drum 15" to 22" in diameter, 12" to 18" deep, without snares, played with snare sticks

Timbre: a battle drum or the characteristic funeral drum

Snare Drum

Description: double-headed drum 13" to 18" in diameter and 6" to 10" deep; played with wooden (snare) sticks; can be played with snares on or off

Timbre: The snares (thin metal wires drawn across the bottom of the drum) produce a sharp, sizzling sound. Effective soft for subtle accents, subdued rhythmical effects; or loud for martial rhythms and heavy accents.

Piccolo Snare Drum

Description: same as snare drum except it is only about 2" to 3" deep

Timbre: played softly, it produces a soft tapping sound (like a distant military memory); loud, it produces a hard staccato sound

Gong (Tam Tam)

Description: a large brass disc that is 18" to 60" in diameter and is hung vertically; played with hard rubber beater

Timbre: lush, resonant sustaining tone evoking Asian associations; effective loud or soft

Tambourine

Description: A 10"–diameter hoop of wood with a leather head on one side and with many small metallic bangles loosely attached to frame. Held in one hand, it can either be shaken or struck with other hand.

Timbre: when struck, it sounds like a small snare drum; when shaken, the small metal pieces set up an exciting, jangling sound

Temple Blocks

Description: set of four hollow wooden spheres (graded from 4" to 8" in diameter) set in a stand and struck with snare sticks

Timbre: although none produce definable pitch, each has an attractive resonant sound that is recognizably higher or lower than the others

Triangle

Description: a metal triangle, each side being 4" to 11" long; activated by a metal beater

Timbre: a penetrating metal-on-metal sonority; when rolled (struck as rapidly as possible), it sets up a brilliant energetic sound; it is also an effective soft accent

Woodblock

Description: an oblong, wooden block (about 8" x 3" x 2") with a slit in it, struck with snare sticks

Timbre: a wood-on-wood sound with minimal resonance

Note: This century has seen a proliferation of unpitched percussion instruments, most being Western adaptations of ethnic instruments. None have as yet achieved sufficient general utility to warrant inclusion in a general orchestration text.

CHORAL SECTIONS

Range:

Soprano:

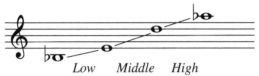

Low   Middle   High

Alto:

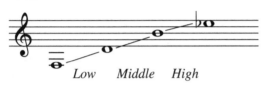

Low   Middle   High

Tenor:

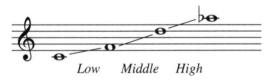

Low   Middle   High

Baritone:

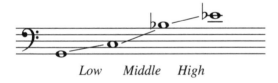

Low   Middle   High

Bass:

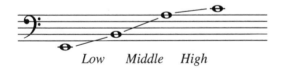

Low   Middle   High

Transposition: all sound as written except tenor which sounds an octave lower than written

Characteristics: regarding all sections, the low register is weak, but has good quality; the mid-range is secure and controlled, while the top is projected and resonant, becoming slightly pinched at the upper extremity

Note: These ranges refer to choristers in say a capable community chorus, ages ranging from 25-60. Collegiate singers would have an additional note or two at the top end, losing possibly a note at the bottom.

NOTES

_____
_____
_____
_____
_____
_____
_____
_____
_____
_____
_____
_____
_____
_____
_____
_____
_____
_____
_____
_____
_____
_____
_____
_____
_____
_____
_____
_____
_____
_____
_____
_____
_____
_____
_____
_____
_____
_____
_____
_____

ORCHESTRATION
handbook

strings

STRINGS

Characteristics:

- good pitch and volume control throughout range
- normally agile throughout range (except string bass), although arpeggiated passages are clumsy, unless composer is familiar with idiosyncrasies of strings
- use phrase marks as if preparing a vocal part, using these to indicate complete phrases; concertmaster will adapt bowing to reflect composer's intent
- two basic kinds of bowed sound: legato (lyric, connected phrases) and staccato (short separated notes), the first indicated by phrase marks, the second by a dot over each note

Special effects:

Am frosch: played near the nut of the bow producing a harsh accented sound

A punta d'arco: played near point of bow

Arco: literally "bowed"; often indicating end of a pizzicato passage

At the frog: same as "am frosch"

Bowing marks: V = upbow; ⊓ = downbow

Col legno: using the wood side of the bow. Players hate this as it damages bow and is rarely successful. Better to substitute "a punta d'arco, spiccato"

Double stop: producing tone on two strings by drawing bow across both simultaneously

Glissando: sliding between pitches (see symbols section)

Harmonics (natural or true): a soft vibratoless tone produced by exciting overtones, accomplished by touching the string lightly while bowing. Each string has several possible natural harmonics, which are indicated by writing a small "o" over the note. Here are the natural harmonics available on the G string of the violin:

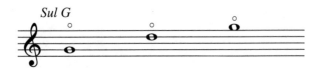

These pitches are the first, second, and third overtones of the "G" fundamental. This concept can be applied to the strings of all bowed instruments, although contrabass harmonics are rarely encountered.

Another way of indicating true harmonics is as follows:

Cautionary note: As there is no consensus regarding natural harmonic symbols (the *Harvard Dictionary* preferring the first, most professional string players preferring the second), there is confusion when these are indicated. It is safer therefore to write false harmonics which produce a more-consistent tone and whose terminology is not confusing.

Harmonics (artificial or false): A soft, vibratoless tone produced by pressing the index finger on the string while lightly touching the same string a fourth higher with another finger. This is indicated by placing a note where the index finger should rest while placing a hollow diamond where the second finger should touch:

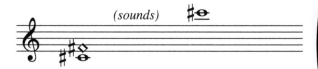

Martellé, Martellato: heavily accented

Mute: A small wooden or plastic piece that fits over the bridge, modifying the resonance so that volume is reduced and tone is more mellow. To indicate, write "sordino" or "mute;" to indicate a return to normal tone, write "senza sordino" or "without mute." Always allow at least two bars rest to insert or remove mute.

Non-Vibrato: indicates absence of vibrato; an even, rather lifeless tone; indicated by "n.v." When returning to normal, write "normale"

Portamento: an exaggerated legato, i.e., a quick glissando between two notes, normally at the discretion of the player

Pizzicato: plucking the string; when returning to bow, indicate "arco" on part

Senza Vibrato: see Non-Vibrato

Sordino (or Con Sordino): see Mute

Spiccato: bouncing the bow off string, rarely indicated on the part

Staccato: very short, bowed notes (see symbols section for notation)

Sul Ponticello: Drawing the bow across string near bridge, producing a thin nasal sound. To return to normal, indicated "normale."

Sul Tasto: Drawing the bow across the string toward the fingerboard, producing a mellow, quiet tone. Another term for this is "flautando." When returning to normal, write "normale."

Sul D, Sul G, etc.: indicates on which string a passage should be played

Tremolo: Rapid alternation of up and down bows on the same pitch (see symbols section)

Trill: Rapid alternation between two pitches (see symbols section)

VIOLIN

Range:　　　　　　　**Harmonic Range:**

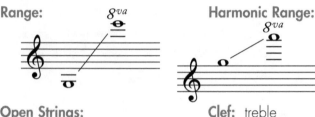

Open Strings:　　　　　　　**Clef:** treble

Transposition: sounds as written

VIOLA

Range:

Harmonic Range:　　　　　　　**Clefs:** alto, treble

Open Strings:

Transposition: sounds as written

CELLO

Range:

Harmonic Range:

Open Strings:

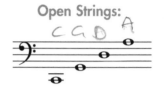

Clefs: bass, tenor, treble

Transposition: sounds as written

Special effects: In addition to the techniques listed under "strings," there is one unique to the cello. Because the body of the cello points away from the player, it is possible to use the index finger as a capo, making four-note chords feasible (either strummed or as an arpeggiated arco); possibilities include major and minor chords, with or without major or minor sevenths. When lowest note of a chord gets above a low G (see last example), the effect becomes rather pinched and loses effectiveness. Here are several examples:

STRING BASS

Range:

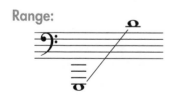

Harmonic Range:

Open Strings:

Clefs: bass, tenor

Transposition: sounds an octave lower than written

[41]

Special effects:

Harmonics: while mechanically possible, are rarely encountered; the sound is not particularly pleasing and has almost no projection

Note: some basses have an extension that extends the lower range to double low C (two notes lower than normal range); but composer must always check to find out if player has such an extension

NOTES

ORCHESTRATION
handbook

symbols in orchestral music

—

volume and tempo indications

—

mood indications

—

directions for execution

—

**sequence of parts on
orchestral score**

—

SYMBOLS USED IN ORCHESTRAL MUSIC
Articulation

Accent mark: indicates a note be accented:

Crescendo mark: indicates increase in volume:

Detaché mark: indicates passage be both accented and sustained; articulated:

Diminuendo mark: indicates an even decrease in volume:

Fermata: holding a note beyond its metrical length (at discretion of performer or conductor):

Glissando: a wavy line indicating an unbroken slide between pitches; practical for clarinet, strings and to a limited extent, trombones:

Louré: a phrased staccato:

Phrase (Expression) mark: an arc indicated notes to be phrased together:

Sforzando: an exaggerated accent, abbreviated "Sf" or "Sfz." "Sfp" indicates sharp accent with soft tail:

Staccato mark: a dot above or below a note indicating it be played short as possible:

Sustain mark: indicates that notes are sustained but not phrased together:

Instrumental effects

Arpeggio: indicates a chord be rolled from lowest note upward unless arrow at bottom, indicates the opposite (on piano, harp, guitar parts):

Tremolo: rapid repetition of the same note (string effect). On percussion same effect is called "roll":

Trill: rapid alternation between written note and neighboring upper note of scale, if music is tonal. Otherwise an accidental at right of trill-sign indicates whether upper note is sharp, natural or flat; indicated thus:

Wider trills between non-adjoining notes indicated as follows:

4

Repeat indications

One-bar repeat mark: repetition of previous measure:

Multiple-bar repeat mark: repeat of more than one bar:

Passage repetition sign: repeat of complete passage:

Come Sopra: bar repeated from earlier in movement; bracketed number tells what bar to repeat:

Da Capo (D.C.): a return to beginning of movement:

Dal Segno (D.S.): a return to the bar marked with a D.S. sign (also see next entry):

Dal Segno sign: after reaching a point in the music marked with a D.S., return to bar marked with this symbol:

Coda sign: after observing a D.S. or a D.C., go from the coda sign ⊕ to an additional piece of music at the end also marked with coda sign:

Note-repetition symbols:

will sound

will sound

will sound

"C" clefs: orchestral writing involves two clefs not normally encountered by non-orchestral musicians, the
"C" clefs. The center of the clef indicates middle
C. These are used by bassoons, violas, celli,
basses and trombones:

alto clef:    *tenor clef:*

Octave-transposition symbols: When placed above
staff, it indicates music should sound an octave
higher than written. Placed below staff, it indicates
music to sound an octave lower:

When returning to concert register, indicate "loco"
on part.
Note: symbol for two-octave transposition is
15ma.

VOLUME INDICATIONS

PPP	=	soft as possible
PP	=	very soft
P	=	soft
MP	=	moderately soft
MF	=	medium volume
F	=	moderately loud
FF	=	very loud
FFF	=	loud as possible

BASIC VOLUME-CHANGE INDICATIONS

Crescendo	=	increase volume
Diminuendo	=	decrease volume

Which may be modified by the following:

Subito	=	suddenly (ahead of term)
Molto	=	a great deal
Assai	=	a great deal (after term)
Poco	=	a little (ahead of term)
Poco a poco	=	gradually

TEMPOS

Tempos are very subjective so the following are approximate. (mm = metronome mark)

Largo	= very very slow	mm	=	54
Adagio	= very slow	mm	=	60
Andante	= slowly	mm	=	66
Andantino	= rather slowly	mm	=	72
Moderato	= moderately	mm	=	80
Allegro molto	= moderate motion	mm	=	88
Allegretto	= with some motion	mm	=	96
Allegro	= rather quickly	mm	=	104
Con moto	= with motion	mm	=	112
Animato	= animated	mm	=	124
Allegro molto	= very fast	mm	=	136
Allegro assai	= very fast	mm	=	144
Celere	= rapidly	mm	=	156
Vivace	= extremely fast	mm	=	168
Vivacissimo	= fast as possible	mm	=	180

TEMPO-CHANGE INDICATIONS

To Reduce Tempo

Allargando	=	broadening, slower (and possibly louder)
Calando	=	slowing; more relaxed
Ritardando	=	slowing down
Rallentando	=	gradually slowing
Meno mosso	=	a little less

To Increase Tempo

Accelerando	=	increase tempo
Affretando	=	accelerating
Stringendo	=	intensifying (faster)
Piu mosso	=	more (faster)

Terms to modify the above (placed ahead of term)

Poco a poco	=	little by little
Poco	=	a little more
Molto	=	a great deal
Non	=	"not" or "without"

Other Terms Modifying Tempo

Ad libitum	=	freely, at discretion of player (also indicates an optional part)
A tempo	=	return to previous tempo
L'Istesso tempo	=	maintain same tempo into the new section
Rubato	=	tempo modified at player's discretion
Slentando	=	a brief ritard
Tenuto	=	a ritard at the end of a phrase
Tempo primo	=	return to original tempo of movement

4

MOOD INDICATIONS*

(usually placed at the beginning of a composition or at a mood change)

Abandono	with abandon, passionately
A capriccio	in a light-hearted manner
Adirato	with anger
Affabile	affably, warm-hearted
Affetuoso	gracefully, with feeling
Agitato	agitated; excited
Amabile	amiably, gracefully
Amore, con	in an amorous mood
Anima, con	spirited, animated
Animato	spirited, animated
Appassionato	passionately
Ardente	fervently, ardently
Ardore, con	with ardor, intensely
Bellicoso	stentorian, bellicose
Bizzaro	strange, bizarre
Brio, con	brilliantly, with spirit
Bruscamente	coarsely, heavily accented
Burlesco	comedic, droll
Calma	calmly
Caloroso	heatedly, fervently
Caminando	relaxed and flowing
Cantando	lyrically, songlike
Comodo	commodiously, expansively
Deciso, con	decisively, boldly
Deliberamente	deliberately
Delirio	out of control; in delirium
Devoto	devout, religiously
Dignita, con	noble, with dignity
Dolce	gently, with affection
Dolente	sadly
Doloroso	with grief
Elegante	elegantly; articulated
Elegia	in an elegiac mood
Energico	vigorously, with energy
Enfatico	with emphasis
Epico	heroic, in an epic manner
Espressivo	with feeling, expressively
Feroce	ferociously
Fervente	fervently, intensely
Festivo	in a festive manner
Forza, con	forcefully
Funerale	funeral-like, gravely

* *Mood indications are always acceptable in English, but Italian terms are understood worldwide.*

Fuoco, con	fiery, impassioned
Furioso	fiercely, with anger
Gaio, con	gaily
Galante	gallantly, spirited
Gaudioso	merry, joyfully
Gentilezzo	in a gracious manner
Giocoso	cheerfully, sportive
Grandioso	grandly, expansively
Grave	slowly, in a solemn manner
Grazia	gracefully
Grottesco	grotesquely
Incalzando	becoming more intense
Irato	angrily
Irresoluto	unsure
Lagrimoso	tearfully, intense sadness
Lamentoso	in a lamenting mood
Legato	in a flowing manner
Leggiero	gracefully, agile
Maestoso	majestically, stately
Marziale	martial, in a military manner
Nobile	in a noble mood
Passione, con	passionately
Patetico	pathetically
Pesante	heavily accented
Piacere, a	at discretion of player or instrumentalist
Religioso	in a religious manner
Risoluto	resolutely
Rustico	in a rustic manner
Scherzando	playfully, impish
Secco	without expression; dry
Semplice	simply, without adornment
Sereno	tranquil, serene
Serioso	in a serious manner
Soave	with elegance, suavely
Sonoro	resonant, sonorous
Spirio, con	spirited, energetic
Teneramente	tenderly
Tranquillo	calmly, tranquilly
Umore, con	humorously
Violente	violent
Vitamente	exuberantly

4

DIRECTIONS FOR EXECUTION

(Normally placed on an individual part)

Accento	accented
Acciaccato	brusquely, forcefully
Ad libitum	at player's discretion
Agevole	lightly, smoothly
Agilita	with agility
Articulato	articulated
Bruscamente	coarsely, harshly
Cuivré	indication to brass player to play with forced brassy tone
Desto	in a sprightly manner
Legato	lyrically, flowing
Loco	indicates a return to written register, after an 8va... passage
Marcato, ben	in strict time
Piacere	at player's discretion
Preciso	exactly as written
Secco	without expression, dry
Sotto voce	at half voice (softly)
Staccato	indicates notes be played as short as possible
Stentando	loud, harsh
Volante	at player's discretion

TRADITIONAL SEQUENCE OF PARTS AS THEY APPEAR ON AN ORCHESTRAL SCORE

Flute 1

Flute 2
(Piccolo)

Oboe 1

Oboe 2
(English Horn)

Clarinet 1

Clarinet 2
(Bass Clarinet)

Saxophones
(1-4 staves)

Bassoon 1

Bassoon 2
(Contra Bsn.)

Horns
1 3
2 4

Trumpet 1

Trumpet 2

Tenor
Trombone
1 2

Bass Trombone
Tuba

Keyboard
(or harp)

Timpani

Percussion 1
(pitched)

Percussion 2
(unpitched)

Electric
Guitar

Electric
Bass

Chorus
(1-4 staves)

Violins
1
2

Viola

Cello

Bass

NOTES

_____
_____
_____
_____
_____
_____
_____
_____
_____
_____
_____
_____
_____
_____
_____
_____
_____
_____
_____
_____
_____
_____
_____
_____
_____
_____
_____
_____
_____
_____
_____
_____
_____
_____
_____
_____
_____
_____
_____
_____
_____
_____
_____
_____
_____
_____

ORCHESTRATION
handbook

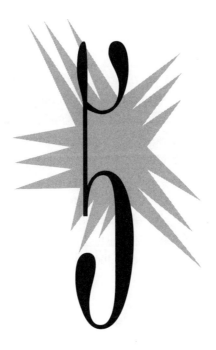

click tracks

—

conversion charts

—

CLICK TRACKS

The most reliable control of tempo in scoring is the click track, a series of audible pops fed by earphones to conductor and players, establishing a predetermined tempo. Take after take, tempo remains constant, musical changes and accents falling as planned. Clicks are useful if players are spread out, if tempo is fast or rhythms complex; but it fails to allow for a musical ebb and flow if the mood is lyrical.

Originally clicks were produced by a loop of film with holes punched in it passing through an optical reader. Today, however we use a digital metronome normally calibrated with both metronome tempos and click settings.

The following tables correlate metronome tempos to clicks and give elapsed time for a series of bars in 2/4, 3/4 and 4/4 at a variety of tempos. If more time is needed than that provided in the tables, use multiples.

Note that one-bar timings are $1/10^{th}$ of the ten-bar timings, *rounded off*. Hence, multiplying any one-bar timing by ten will give a different figure than the ten-bar timing. The ten-bar timing is always the more accurate.

ACCUMULATED TIMING TABLE FOR DIGITAL METRONOME (CLICK MACHINE)

metronome	click	meter	1 bar	2 bars	3 bars	4 bars	5 bars	10 bars
54	26-5	2/4	:02.2	:04.4	:06.7	:08.9	:11.1	:22.2
		3/4	:03.3	:06.7	:10.0	:13.3	:16.7	:33.3
		4/4	:04.4	:08.9	:13.3	:17.8	:22.2	:44.5
56	25-6	2/4	:02.1	:04.3	:06.4	:08.6	:10.7	:21.5
		3/4	:03.2	:06.4	:09.6	:12.9	:16.1	:32.2
		4/4	:04.3	:08.6	:12.9	:17.1	:21.4	:42.9
58	24-7	2/4	:02.1	:04.1	:06.2	:08.3	:10.4	:20.7
		3/4	:03.1	:06.2	:09.3	:12.4	:15.6	:31.1
		4/4	:04.1	:08.3	:12.4	:16.6	:20.7	:41.5
60	24-0	2/4	:02.0	:04.0	:06.0	:08.0	:10.0	:20.0
		3/4	:03.0	:06.0	:09.0	:12.0	:15.0	:30.0
		4/4	:04.0	:08.0	:12.0	:16.0	:20.0	:40.0
62	23-2	2/4	:01.9	:03.9	:05.8	:07.7	:09.7	:19.4
		3/4	:02.9	:05.8	:08.7	:11.6	:14.5	:29.1
		4/4	:03.9	:07.8	:11.6	:15.5	:19.4	:38.8

5

ACCUMULATED TIMING TABLE FOR DIGITAL METRONOME (CLICK MACHINE)

metronome	click	meter	1 bar	2 bars	3 bars	4 bars	5 bars	10 bars
64	22-5	2/4	:01.9	:03.8	:05.7	:07.6	:09.4	:18.9
		3/4	:02.8	:05.7	:08.5	:11.3	:14.2	:28.4
		4/4	:03.8	:07.6	:11.3	:15.1	:18.9	:37.8
66	21-7	2/4	:01.8	:03.6	:05.5	:07.3	:09.1	:18.2
		3/4	:02.7	:05.6	:08.2	:10.9	:13.7	:27.4
		4/4	:03.6	:07.3	:10.9	:14.6	:18.2	:36.5
68	21-1	2/4	:01.8	:03.5	:05.3	:07.0	:08.8	:17.6
		3/4	:02.6	:05.3	:07.9	:10.6	:13.2	:26.4
		4/4	:03.5	:07.0	:10.6	:14.1	:17.6	:35.2
70	20-4	2/4	:01.7	:03.4	:05.1	:06.8	:08.5	:17.1
		3/4	:02.6	:05.1	:07.7	:10.2	:12.8	:25.6
		4/4	:03.4	:06.8	:10.2	:13.7	:17.1	:34.2
72	20-0	2/4	:01.7	:03.3	:05.0	:06.7	:08.3	:16.7
		3/4	:02.5	:05.0	:07.5	:10.0	:12.5	:25.0
		4/4	:03.3	:06.7	:10.0	:13.3	:16.7	:33.3

ACCUMULATED TIMING TABLE FOR DIGITAL METRONOME (CLICK MACHINE)

metronome	click	meter	1 bar	2 bars	3 bars	4 bars	5 bars	10 bars
74	19-4	2/4	:01.6	:03.2	:04.9	:06.5	:08.1	:16.3
		3/4	:02.4	:04.9	:07.3	:09.7	:12.2	:24.4
		4/4	:03.2	:06.5	:09.7	:13.0	:16.3	:32.5
76	18-7	2/4	:01.6	:03.1	:04.7	:06.3	:07.9	:15.7
		3/4	:02.4	:04.7	:07.1	:09.4	:11.8	:23.6
		4/4	:03.1	:06.3	:09.4	:12.6	:15.7	:31.5
78	18-4	2/4	:01.5	:03.1	:04.6	:06.1	:07.7	:15.4
		3/4	:02.3	:04.6	:069	:09.2	:11.6	:23.1
		4/4	:03.1	:06.2	:09.2	:12.3	:15.4	:30.8
80	18-0	2/4	:01.5	:03.0	:04.5	:06.0	:07.5	:15.0
		3/4	:02.3	:04.5	:06.8	:09.0	:11.3	:22.5
		4/4	:03.0	:06.0	:09.0	:12.0	:15.0	:30.0
82	17-4	2/4	:01.5	:02.9	:04.4	:05.8	:07.3	:14.6
		3/4	:02.2	:04.4	:06.6	:08.7	:10.9	:21.9
		4/4	:02.9	:05.8	:08.7	:11.7	:14.6	:29.2

5

ACCUMULATED TIMING TABLE FOR DIGITAL METRONOME (CLICK MACHINE)

metronome	click	meter	1 bar	2 bars	3 bars	4 bars	5 bars	10 bars
84	17-1	2/4	:01.4	:02.8	:04.3	:05.7	:07.2	:14.3
		3/4	:02.1	:04.3	:06.4	:08.6	:10.7	:21.4
		4/4	:02.9	:05.7	:08.6	:11.4	:14.3	:28.5
86	16-6	2/4	:01.4	:02.8	:04.2	:05.6	:07.0	:14.0
		3/4	:02.1	:04.3	:06.3	:08.4	:10.5	:20.9
		4/4	:02.8	:05.6	:08.4	:11.1	:13.9	:27.9
88	16-3	2/4	:01.4	:02.7	:04.1	:05.5	:06.8	:13.7
		3/4	:02.0	:04.1	:06.1	:08.2	:10.2	:20.5
		4/4	:02.7	:05.5	:08.2	:10.9	:13.7	:27.3
90	16-0	2/4	:01.3	:02.7	:04.0	:05.3	:06.7	:13.3
		3/4	:02.0	:04.0	:06.0	:08.0	:10.0	:20.0
		4/4	:02.7	:05.3	:08.0	:10.7	:13.3	:26.7
92	15-5	2/4	:01.3	:02.6	:03.9	:05.2	:06.5	:13.1
		3/4	:02.0	:03.9	:05.9	:07.8	:09.8	:19.6
		4/4	:02.6	:05.2	:07.8	:10.4	:13.1	:26.1

ACCUMULATED TIMING TABLE FOR DIGITAL METRONOME (CLICK MACHINE)

metronome	click	meter	1 bar	2 bars	3 bars	4 bars	5 bars	10 bars
94	15-2	2/4	:01.3	:02.5	:03.8	:05.1	:06.4	:12.7
		3/4	:01.9	:03.8	:05.7	:07.6	:09.5	:15.1
		4/4	:02.5	:05.1	:07.6	:10.1	:12.7	:25.4
96	15-0	2/4	:01.3	:02.5	:03.7	:05.0	:06.3	:12.5
		3/4	:01.9	:03.8	:05.6	:07.5	:09.4	:18.8
		4/4	:02.5	:05.0	:07.5	:10.0	:12.5	:25.0
98	14-6	2/4	:01.2	:02.5	:03.7	:04.9	:06.1	:12.3
		3/4	:01.8	:03.7	:05.5	:07.4	:09.2	:18.4
		4/4	:02.5	:04.9	:07.4	:09.8	:12.3	:24.6
100	14-4	2/4	:01.2	:02.4	:03.6	:04.8	:06.0	:12.1
		3/4	:01.8	:03.6	:05.4	:07.2	:09.0	:18.1
		4/4	:02.4	:04.8	:07.2	:09.7	:12.1	:24.2
102	14-1	2/4	:01.2	:02.4	:03.5	:04.7	:05.9	:11.8
		3/4	:01.8	:03.5	:05.3	:07.1	:08.8	:17.7
		4/4	:02.4	:04.7	:07.1	:09.4	:11.8	:23.5

ACCUMULATED TIMING TABLE FOR DIGITAL METRONOME (CLICK MACHINE)

metronome	click	meter	1 bar	2 bars	3 bars	4 bars	5 bars	10 bars
104	13-7	2/4	:01.2	:02.2	:03.5	:04.6	:05.8	:11.6
		3/4	:01.7	:03.5	:05.2	:06.9	:08.7	:17.3
		4/4	:02.3	:04.6	:06.9	:09.2	:11.6	:23.1
106	13-4	2/4	:01.1	:02.3	:03.4	:04.5	:05.6	:11.3
		3/4	:01.7	:03.4	:05.1	:06.8	:08.4	:16.9
		4/4	:02.3	:04.5	:06.6	:09.0	:11.3	:22.5
108	13-2	2/4	:01.1	:02.2	:03.3	:04.4	:05.5	:11.0
		3/4	:01.7	:03.3	:05.0	:06.6	:08.3	:16.6
		4/4	:02.2	:04.4	:06.6	:08.8	:11.0	:22.1
110	13-0	2/4	:01.1	:02.2	:03.2	:04.3	:05.4	:10.8
		3/4	:01.6	:03.2	:04.9	:06.5	:08.1	:16.2
		4/4	:02.2	:04.3	:06.5	:08.7	:10.8	:21.7
112	12-7	2/4	:01.1	:02.1	:03.2	:04.3	:05.4	:10.7
		3/4	:01.6	:03.2	:04.8	:06.4	:08.0	:16.1
		4/4	:02.1	:04.3	:06.4	:08.6	:10.7	:21.5

ACCUMULATED TIMING TABLE FOR DIGITAL METRONOME (CLICK MACHINE)

metronome	click	meter	1 bar	2 bars	3 bars	4 bars	5 bars	10 bars
114	12-5	2/4	:01.1	:02.1	:03.2	:04.2	:05.3	:10.6
		3/4	:01.6	:03.2	:04.7	:06.3	:07.9	:15.8
		4/4	:02.1	:04.2	:06.3	:08.4	:10.6	:21.1
116	12-3	2/4	:01.0	:02.1	:03.1	:04.1	:05.2	:10.3
		3/4	:01.5	:03.1	:04.6	:06.2	:07.7	:15.5
		4/4	:02.1	:04.1	:06.2	:08.2	:10.3	:20.6
118	12-1	2/4	:01.0	:02.0	:03.0	:04.0	:05.5	:10.1
		3/4	:01.5	:03.0	:04.5	:06.1	:07.6	:15.2
		4/4	:02.0	:04.0	:06.1	:08.1	:10.1	:20.2
120	12-0	2/4	:01.0	:02.0	:03.0	:04.0	:05.0	:10.0
		3/4	:01.5	:03.0	:04.5	:06.0	:07.5	:15.0
		4/4	:02.0	:04.0	:06.0	:08.0	:10.0	:20.0
124	11-5	2/4	:01.0	:01.9	:02.9	:03.	:04.9	:09.7
		3/4	:01.5	:02.9	:04.4	:05.8	:07.3	:14.6
		4/4	:01.9	:03.9	:05.8	:07.8	:09.7	:19.5

5

ACCUMULATED TIMING TABLE FOR DIGITAL METRONOME (CLICK MACHINE)

metronome	click	meter	1 bar	2 bars	3 bars	4 bars	5 bars	10 bars
128	11-2	2/4	:00.9	:01.9	:02.8	:03.7	:04.7	:09.4
		3/4	:01.4	:02.8	:04.2	:05.6	:07.0	:14.1
		4/4	:01.9	:03.8	:05.6	:07.5	:09.4	:18.8
132	10-7	2/4	:00.9	:01.8	:02.7	:03.6	:04.5	:09.1
		3/4	:01.3	:02.7	:04.1	:05.4	:06.8	:13.6
		4/4	:01.8	:03.6	:05.4	:07.2	:09.1	:18.1
136	10-5	2/4	:00.9	:01.8	:02.7	:03.6	:04.4	:08.9
		3/4	:01.3	:02.7	:04.0	:05.3	:06.7	:13.4
		4/4	:01.8	:03.6	:05.3	:07.1	:08.9	:17.8
140	10-3	2/4	:00.8	:01.7	:02.6	:03.5	:04.3	:08.7
		3/4	:01.3	:02.6	:03.9	:05.2	:06.5	:13.0
		4/4	:01.7	:03.5	:05.2	:06.9	:08.6	:17.3
144	10-0	2/4	:00.8	:01.7	:02.5	:03.3	:04.2	:08.3
		3/4	:01.3	:02.5	:03.8	:05.0	:06.3	:12.5
		4/4	:01.7	:03.5	:05.0	:06.7	:08.3	:16.7

ACCUMULATED TIMING TABLE FOR DIGITAL METRONOME (CLICK MACHINE)

metronome	click	meter	1 bar	2 bars	3 bars	4 bars	5 bars	10 bars
148	9-6	2/4	:00.8	:01.6	:02.4	:03.2	:04.1	:08.1
		3/4	:01.2	:02.4	:03.7	:04.9	:06.1	:12.2
		4/4	:01.6	:03.3	:04.9	:06.5	:08.1	:16.2
152	9-4	2/4	:00.8	:01.6	:02.4	:03.2	:04.0	:07.9
		3/4	:01.2	:02.4	:03.6	:04.8	:05.9	:11.9
		4/4	:01.6	:03.2	:04.8	:06.3	:07.9	:15.8
156	9-2	2/4	:00.8	:01.5	:02.3	:03.1	:03.8	:07.7
		3/4	:01.2	:02.2	:03.5	:04.6	:05.8	:11.6
		4/4	:01.5	:03.1	:04.6	:06.2	:07.7	:15.4
160	9-0	2/4	:00.7	:01.5	:02.3	:03.0	:03.8	:07.5
		3/4	:01.1	:02.3	:03.4	:04.5	:05.6	:11.3
		4/4	:01.5	:03.0	:04.5	:06.0	:07.5	:15.0
164	8-7	2/4	:00.7	:01.5	:02.2	:03.0	:03.7	:07.4
		3/4	:01.1	:02.2	:03.3	:04.4	:05.6	:11.1
		4/4	:01.5	:03.0	:04.4	:05.9	:07.4	:14.8

ACCUMULATED TIMING TABLE FOR DIGITAL METRONOME (CLICK MACHINE)

metronome	click	meter	1 bar	2 bars	3 bars	4 bars	5 bars	10 bars
168	8-5	2/4	:00.7	:01.4	:02.2	:02.9	:03.6	:07.2
		3/4	:01.1	:02.2	:03.3	:04.3	:05.4	:10.9
		4/4	:01.4	:02.9	:04.3	:05.8	:07.2	:14.5
172	8-3	2/4	:00.7	:01.4	:02.1	:02.8	:03.5	:07.0
		3/4	:01.0	:02.1	:03.1	:04.2	:05.2	:10.5
		4/4	:01.4	:02.8	:04.2	:05.6	:07.0	:14.0
176	8-1	2/4	:00.7	:01.4	:02.0	:02.7	:03.4	:06.8
		3/4	:01.0	:02.0	:03.0	:04.1	:05.1	:10.2
		4/4	:01.4	:02.7	:04.1	:05.4	:06.8	:13.5
180	8-0	2/4	:00.7	:01.3	:02.0	:02.7	:03.4	:06.7
		3/4	:01.0	:02.0	:03.0	:04.0	:05.0	:10.0
		4/4	:01.3	:02.7	:04.0	:05.3	:06.7	:13.3
184	7-6	2/4	:00.6	:01.3	:01.9	:02.6	:03.2	:06.5
		3/4	:01.0	:01.9	:02.9	:03.9	:04.8	:09.7
		4/4	:01.3	:02.6	:03.9	:05.2	:06.5	:12.9
188	7-5	2/4	:00.6	:01.3	:01.9	:02.6	:03.2	:06.4
		3/4	:01.0	:01.9	:02.9	:03.8	:04.8	:09.6
		4/4	:01.3	:02.6	:03.8	:05.1	:06.4	:12.8

CONVERSION CHART: 16mm film

(If a half-foot is involved, add :00 5/6 to timing)

Feet	Seconds	Feet	Seconds	Feet	Seconds
1	:01 2/3	37	1:01 2/3	73	2:01 2/3
2	:03 1/3	38	1:03 1/3	74	2:03 1/3
3	:05	39	1:05	75	2:05
4	:06 2/3	40	1:06 2/3	76	2:06 2/3
5	:08 1/3	41	1:08 1/3	77	2:08 1/3
6	:10	42	1:10	78	2:10
7	:11 2/3	43	1:11 2/3	79	2:11 2/3
8	:13 1/3	44	1:13 1/3	80	2:13 1/3
9	:15	45	1:15	81	2:15
10	:16 2/3	46	1:16 2/3	82	2:16 2/3
11	:18 1/3	47	1:18 1/3	83	2:18 1/3
12	:20	48	1:20	84	2:20
13	:21 2/3	49	1:21 2/3	85	2:21 2/3
14	:23 1/3	50	1:23 1/3	86	2:23 1/3
15	:25	51	1:25	87	2:25
16	:26 2/3	52	1:26 2/3	88	2:26 2/3
17	:28 1/3	53	1:28 1/3	89	2:28 1/3
18	:30	54	1:30	90	2:30
19	:31 2/3	55	1:31 2/3	91	2:31 2/3
20	:33 1/3	56	1:33 1/3	92	2:33 1/3
21	:35	57	1:35	93	2:35
22	:36 2/3	58	1:36 2/3	94	2:36 2/3
23	:38 1/3	59	1:38 1/3	95	2:38 1/3
24	:40	60	1:40	96	2:40
25	:41 2/3	61	1:41 2/3	97	2:41 2/3
26	:43 1/3	62	1:43 1/3	98	2:43 1/3
27	:45	63	1:45	99	2:45
28	:46 2/3	64	1:46 2/3	100	2:46 2/3
29	:48 1/3	65	1:48 1/3	101	2:48 1/3
30	:50	66	1:50	102	2:50
31	:51 2/3	67	1:51 2/3	103	2:51 2/3
32	:53 1/3	68	1:53 1/3	104	2:53 1/3
33	:55	69	1:55	105	2:55
34	:56 2/3	70	1:56 2/3	106	2:56 2/3
35	:58 1/3	71	1:58 1/3	107	2:58 1/3
36	1:00	72	2:00	108	3:00

Note: If confronted with a 16mm film lacking a timing code, this chart will convert footages to seconds and minutes.

CONVERSION CHART: 35mm film

Feet	Seconds	Feet	Seconds	Feet	Seconds
1	:00 2/3	37	:24 2/3	73	:48 2/3
2	:01 1/3	38	:25 1/3	74	:49 1/3
3	:02	39	:26	75	:50
4	:02 2/3	40	:26 2/3	76	:50 2/3
5	:03 1/3	41	:27 1/3	77	:51 1/3
6	:04	42	:28	78	:52
7	:04 2/3	43	:28 2/3	79	:52 2/3
8	:05 1/3	44	:29 1/3	80	:53 1/3
9	:06	45	:30	81	:54
10	:06 2/3	46	:30 2/3	82	:54 2/3
11	:07 1/3	47	:31 1/3	83	:55 1/3
12	:08	48	:32	84	:56
13	:08 2/3	49	:32 2/3	85	:56 2/3
14	:09 1/3	50	:33 1/3	86	:57 1/3
15	:10	51	:34	87	:58
16	:10 2/3	52	:34 2/3	88	:58 2/3
17	:11 1/3	53	:35 1/3	89	:59 1/3
18	:12	54	:36	90	1:00
19	:12 2/3	55	:36 2/3	91	1:00 2/3
20	:13 1/3	56	:37 1/3	92	1:01 1/3
21	:14	57	:38	93	1:02
22	:14 2/3	58	:38 2/3	94	1:02 2/3
23	:15 1/3	59	:39 1/3	95	1:03 1/3
24	:16	60	:40	96	1:04
25	:16 2/3	61	:40 2/3	97	1:04 2/3
26	:17 1/3	62	:41 1/3	98	1:05 1/3
27	:18	63	:42	99	1:06
28	:18 2/3	64	:42 2/3	100	1:06 2/3
29	:19 1/3	65	:43 1/3	101	1:07 1/3
30	:20	66	:44	102	1:08
31	:20 2/3	67	:44 2/3	103	1:08 2/3
32	:21 1/3	68	:45 1/3	104	1:09 1/3
33	:22	69	:46	105	1:10
34	:22 2/3	70	:46 2/3	106	1:10 2/3
35	:23 1/3	71	:47 1/3	107	1:11 1/3
36	:24	72	:48	108	1:12

Note: If confronted with a 35mm film lacking a timing code, this chart will convert footages to seconds and minutes.

CONVERSION CHART: 35mm film

Feet	Seconds	Feet	Seconds	Feet	Seconds
109	1:12 2/3	145	1:36 2/3	181	2:00 2/3
110	1:13 1/3	146	1:37 1/3	182	2:01 1/3
111	1:14	147	1:38	183	2:02
112	1:14 2/3	148	1:38 2/3	184	2:02 2/3
113	1:15 1/3	149	1:39 1/3	185	2:03 1/3
114	1:16	150	1:40	186	2:04
115	1:16 2/3	151	1:40 2/3	187	2:04 2/3
116	1:17 1/3	152	1:41 1/3	188	2:05 1/3
117	1:18	153	1:42	189	2:06
118	1:18 2/3	154	1:42 2/3	190	2:06 2/3
119	1:19 1/3	155	1:43 1/3	191	2:07 1/3
120	1:20	156	1:44	192	2:08
121	1:20 2/3	157	1:44 2/3	193	2:08 2/3
122	1:21 1/3	158	1:45 1/3	194	2:09 1/3
123	1:22	159	1:46	195	2:10
124	1:22 2/3	160	1:46 2/3	196	2:10 2/3
125	1:23 1/3	161	1:47 1/3	197	2:11 1/3
126	1:24	162	1:48	198	2:12
127	1:24 2/3	163	1:48 2/3	199	2:12 2/3
128	1:25 1/3	164	1:49 1/3	200	2:13 1/3
129	1:26	165	1:50	201	2:14
130	1:26 2/3	166	1:50 2/3	202	2:14 2/3
131	1:27 1/3	167	1:51 1/3	203	2:15 1/3
132	1:28	168	1:52	204	2:16
133	1:28 2/3	169	1:52 2/3	205	2:16 2/3
134	1:29 1/3	170	1:53 1/3	206	2:17 1/3
135	1:30	171	1:54	207	2:18
136	1:30 2/3	172	1:54 2/3	208	2:18 2/3
137	1:31 1/3	173	1:55 1/3	209	2:19 1/3
138	1:32	174	1:56	210	2:20
139	1:32 2/3	175	1:56 2/3	211	2:20 2/3
140	1:33 1/3	176	1:57 1/3	212	2:21 1/3
141	1:34	177	1:58	213	2:22
142	1:34 2/3	178	1:58 2/3	214	2:22 2/3
143	1:35 1/3	179	1:59 1/3	215	2:23 1/3
144	1:36	180	2:00	216	2:24

5

CONVERSION CHART: 35mm film

Feet	Seconds		Feet	Seconds		Feet	Seconds	
217	2:24	2/3	253	2:48	2/3	289	3:12	2/3
218	2:25	1/3	254	2:49	1/3	290	3:13	1/3
219	2:26		255	2:50		291	3:14	
220	2:26	2/3	256	2:50	2/3	292	3:14	2/3
221	2:27	1/3	257	2:51	1/3	293	3:15	1/3
222	2:28		258	2:52		294	3:16	
223	2:28	2/3	259	2:52	2/3	295	3:16	2/3
224	2:29	1/3	260	2:53	1/3	296	3:17	1/3
225	2:30		261	2:54		297	3:18	
226	2:30	2/3	262	2:54	2/3	298	3:18	2/3
227	2:31	1/3	263	2:55	1/3	299	3:19	1/3
228	2:32		264	2:56		300	3:20	
229	2:32	2/3	265	2:56	2/3	301	3:20	2/3
230	2:33	1/3	266	2:57	1/3	302	3:21	1/3
231	2:34		267	2:58		303	3:22	
232	2:34	2/3	268	2:58	2/3	304	3:22	2/3
233	2:35	1/3	269	2:50	1/3	305	3:23	1/3
234	2:36		270	3:00		306	3:24	
235	2:36	2/3	271	3:00	2/3	307	3:24	2/3
236	2:37	1/3	272	3:01	1/3	308	3:25	1/3
237	2:38		273	3:02		309	3:26	
238	2:38	2/3	274	3:02	2/3	310	3:26	2/3
239	2:39	1/3	275	3:03	1/3	311	3:27	1/3
240	2:40		276	3:04		312	3:28	
241	2:40	2/3	277	3:04	2/3	313	3:28	2/3
242	2:41	1/3	278	3:05	1/3	314	3:29	1/3
243	2:42		279	3:06		315	3:30	
244	2:42	2/3	280	3:06	2/3	316	3:30	2/3
245	2:43	1/3	281	3:07	1/3	317	3:31	1/3
246	2:44		282	3:08		318	3:32	
247	2:44	2/3	283	3:08	2/3	319	3:32	2/3
248	2:45	1/3	284	3:09	1/3	320	3:33	1/3
249	2:46		285	3:10		321	3:34	
250	2:46	2/3	286	3:10	2/3	322	3:35	2/3
251	2:47	1/3	287	3:11	1/3	323	3:35	1/3
252	2:48		288	3:12		324	3:36	

NOTES

5

[71]

About the Author

Born and raised in Southern California, Don B. Ray
got his B.A. at UCLA and his M.A. from
California State University, Long Beach. In 1956
he joined the CBS Network Music Department,
where he remained until his retirement. As Music
Supervisor, he was responsible for the music on
Playhouse 90, *The Twilight Zone*, *Gunsmoke*,
Rawhide, and *Hawaii Five-O*, the latter bringing
an Emmy® nomination for Best Dramatic Score
in 1974.

In 1980 he created the Film Scoring Program at
UCLA's Department of the Arts (and was named
Outstanding Instructor in that department in
1984). During this period, he was also a guest
lecturer at the University of London. In 1997, he
was invited to recreate the UCLA program in
Dublin, Ireland. He now spends part of each year
in Dublin. Ray is married, has one son, and lives
in Southern California.